D1297523

HUNTER'S LOG

HUNTER'S LOG

Field Notes

1988 – 2011

by

TIMOTHY MURPHY

Foreword by James R. Babb

Illustrated by Eldridge Hardie

The Dakota Institute Press
of the Lewis & Clark Fort Mandan Foundation

*Library of Congress Control Number 2011937808
ISBN-13 978-0-9825597-9-6 (Hardcover)
ISBN-13 978-0-9834059-0-0 (Paperback)*

*Distributed by The University of Oklahoma Press
Created, produced and designed in the United States of America
Printed in Canada*

*Book layout and design by:
Margaret McCullough corvusdesignstudio.com*

*The paper in this book meets the guidelines for permanence and
durability of the Committee of Production Guidelines for Book
Longevity of the Council on Library Resources.
10 9 8 7 6 5 4 3 2 1*

Cover Image: *Pheasant Hunters* by Eldridge Hardie
Publication of this book and acquisition of Eldridge Hardie art made
possible by a generous contribution from Alvera Bergquist

The Dakota Institute Press
of the Lewis & Clark Fort Mandan Foundation
2576 8th St South West . Post Office Box 607
Washburn, North Dakota 58577
www.fortmandan.com
1.877.462.8535

To Eldridge Hardie

Cave paintings at Lascaux,
and what had man to fear,
thousands of years ago?
The wolf drawn from its near
starvation in the snow?

You have a muscular way
of wading up a stream
or quartering the hay—
the way you draw and dream,
saying what I would say.

CONTENTS

II. ELMWOOD'S MAUD GONNE

III. ELMWOOD'S BOLD FENIAN

IV. EPILOGUE: A HUNTING SEASON

FOREWORD

To the great mass of educated humanity, poetry has become something mandatorily memorized and then promptly discarded, leaving behind dusty cobwebs stuck with the husks of paths less taken and one if by land and cannons to the left of me and candles burned at both ends, along with, of course, the proclivities of certain men from Nantucket.

There's no shortage of published poetry these days. What there's a shortage of are people who read it. Which begs the question: Have people left poetry, or has poetry simply left people?

Where today is that brand of wordsmithing Matthew Arnold called natural magic? What has happened to the breed of poet Washington Irving described as spreading "the magic of his mind over the very face of Nature, to give to things and places a charm and character not their own, and to turn this 'working-day world' into a perfect fairy-land?"

Good luck finding the working-day world in much of modern poetry, written mostly by Masters of Fine Arts to impress, confound, or amplify other Masters of Fine Arts, perhaps in hopes of profiting from poetry by the sole remaining path: participating in the manufacture of still more Masters of Fine Arts. The face of nature, I sometimes suspect, has wandered off into a hexametric résumé and died of disappointment.

I don't mean to dismiss the modern poetry establishment so much as simply to observe that it mostly dismisses my particular working-day world. I live in a world of fishing rods and pickup trucks and plowed furrows and felled trees; of rising trout and hatching mayflies and the sun's low glare on iron-gray water; of guns and dogs and shadows falling across apple orchards planted, tended, and ultimately abandoned by distant ancestors; of the delicate step of a deer and the whirr of grouse wings and the shotgun's push against a shoulder; of the too-frequent misses and the occasional good shots, and the flutter of feathers and the unrestrained approval of a hard-working dog; of the unforgettable scent and taste and tangible connection to The Meaning Of It All through a grouse reverently devoured before a living fire.

Tim Murphy writes of this world as few do—as an act of natural magic, the natural world seen through the eyes of a participant with mud and blood beneath his nails, a world of grain drills and ripe barley and fields going feral through forces both economic and climactic. Through his words live the weight of a North Dakota winter, the arctic vastness of the Northwest Territories, the birth and career and inevitable death of our partners in this particular life, both two-legged and four: a working-day world in verse from someone who lives there and doesn't simply visit on nice weekends.

"In autumn I subsist on what I shoot," Murphy writes. When the season passes and until another comes again, we of his world can subsist on what he has written, and what the great Eldridge Hardie has illustrated, an invitation into a world far removed from the halls of academia, a permanent hall pass into the corn rows and the sun and the rain and the heat and the cold, forever enlivened by the whir of wings, the wet noses of dogs, and the shotgun's delicious blast.

James R. Babb, Editor
Gray's Sporting Journal

PREFACE

I believe my father first took me afield when I was about seven. I remember the thrill when he had me drive a 1956 Chevy station wagon from one end of a stubble field to another, so the men would have return transportation after their walk. I vividly recall my first pheasant, goose, and duck. We didn't hunt with dogs. Nowadays I would rather go afield without my Winchester than without my dog. I acquired my first lab in 1986, when I was thirty-five. I have now been blessed with four of these peerless creatures.

It was just about that time my father gave me Ortega y Gasset's <u>Meditations on Hunting</u>. That philosopher from Spain taught me many lessons, but the three greatest are these. First, that the killing of the game is a ritual preparation for our own mortality. By 1986 the men who taught me to hunt were many of them at death's door, and my father was a sought-after speaker at funerals. I think I best bring this lesson to bear in my poems, The Blind, Hunting Time, and Pass Shooter. The second is the lesson of Ortega y Gasset's sixth chapter, Suddenly We Hear the Sound of Barking: "With the addition of dogs to beaters and shooters, hunting acquires a certain kind of symphonic majesty." For the final lesson, I ask readers to consider deeply the philosopher's final chapter: "The Hunter, the Alert Man." Hunting teaches us accuracy of observation, and if one is to write about it, or draw it as Eldridge Hardie does so skillfully, accuracy of expression.

Timothy Murphy

I. ELMWOOD'S DIKTYNNA THEA

Pronghorn

February

A coyote hides in a draw
under a bale of straw,
dreaming of gopher mounds
on dusty lekking grounds
where prairie chickens dance,
newborn pronghorns prance
and killdeers caterwaul.
So hunters dream of fall.

Failures of Promise

A flock of crows
found a road-killed ewe
frozen in the snow.
A drowsy bear
dragged a leg-shot deer
to its deadfall lair.
The lamb in the ewe
and the fawn in the doe
were devoured unborn,
and November snows
buried the standing corn.

Diktynna Thea
for Jose Ortega y Gasset

We hunker by the fire
to read a hunter's praise
of Socrates. The blaze
leaps like a dog's desire
when ducks circle a blind,
then gutters and burns low.
Outside the moonlit snow
flows in a bitter wind.
I scratch my bitch's withers.
She sighs for whirring Huns,
cackling cocks, blasting guns
and a mouthful of feathers.

Nothing Goes to Waste

Rearing on spindly legs
a pair of famished stags
nibble our apple twigs
while does heavy with fawn
file from the woods at dawn
and tiptoe across the lawn
to feast on orchard mast
scattered in harvest haste
before the first hard frost.
Nothing goes to waste.

Songs of the North

I. The Weaver

Her loom is bone
and her comb, baleen.
The yarn is wool
from an arctic ox
spun with the down
of eider ducks.
She summons whales,
spotted seals
and narwhals
to a bloodstained beach.
She conjures hunters
blown astray
on the windy reach
of Baffin Bay.
Tidal shallows,
glacial gravel,
stunted willows
and ptarmigan,
she weaves, unravels
and weaves again.

II. The Barrens

The snowy owl
swoops on a vole.
White wolves howl
on a moonlit hill.
But no hunter
waits for the herd
or hears the thunder
of hooves at the ford.
A pox from the South
has emptied the North.

III. Three Foxes

The red fox sleeps in the woods
under a roof of roots.
The long-eared desert fox
dens in the weathered rocks.
But when the blizzards wail
the Arctic fox curls its tail
over its frosty nose
and sleeps in the snows.

IV. Grønland

The last ship sails;
the barley fails.
Only the bones
of the Danes remain.
Marmots peer
from the felsenmeer,
and the wise ravens
at Jakobshavn
breed in the lemming years.

V. Man of the North

I am a wall of rock,
a raucous rookery
where thieving skuas flock.
I am a sunlit sea
where murres and puffins splash
into the tinkling brash.
I am the slaughtered whales,
walruses and seals,
the storm-shredded sails
and bleached, skeletal keels
of whalers run aground
with all hands drowned.

From A Dog Young and Old

I. Obedience

I am the Alpha male,
dispenser of her meat.
With drooping ears and tail
she trembles at my feet.
Leader of the pack,
I growl a wolfish note,
tumble her on her back
and bite her furry throat.

IV. Dog Heaven

Sprawled in the pickup box,
my old bitch is half-dead.
Her slashed teat needs stitches,
her nettled nose twitches,
and nine gutted pheasant cocks
pillow her dreaming head.

Spring Snow

When stoneflies hatch
on the Yellowstone,
browns and rainbows snatch
every feathery fly flown
from the talused banks.
Fish and give thanks.

To a Trout

I whet my hook
beneath a pine,
then with a swish
I loft my line
over a brook
of sparkling wine.
Come little fish,
and we will dine.

Rainbow Trout

Passel o' Pups

Bonny bairnies, black an' fine,
wi yir yivver souks an' ruggs,
will ye be guid hountin dugs
worthy o' yir faither's line?
Will ye busk an' tak them doun,
frantik pairtrick, crouchin grouse,
an' the Deil's ain phaisant louse?
Will ye ding the raibbit broon?
Lak the dun deir ye maun lepe
owre yon scraggy, stany hill
whaur the wund blaws lood an' shrill,
sare an' snell, whaur muckle depe
drifts the snaw. Drink yir fill,
glazie beasties; souk an' slepe.

(in translation)

Pretty babies, black and fine,
with your eager sucks and tugs,
will you be good hunting dogs
worthy of your father's line?
Will you hasten and take them down,
frantic partridge, crouching grouse
and the Devil's own pheasant flush?
Will you smite the rabbit brown?
Like the gray deer you must leap
over yon stony, weedy hill
where the wind blows loud and shrill,
sore and cold, where very deep
drifts the snow. Drink your fill,
glossy beasties. Suck and sleep.

Razing the Woodlot
for Vincent R. Murphy

Here stands the grove our tenant plans to fell.
The homesteaders who planted this tree claim
fled North Dakota when the Dust Bowl came.
Their foursquare farmhouse is a roofless shell;
their tended shelterbelt, a den for fox
and dumpground for machinery and rocks.

The woodlot seeds its pigweed in our loam,
and windstorms topple poplars on the field;
but for a few wasted acres' yield
we'll spare the vixen and her cubs their home
and leave unburied these decaying beams
to teach us the temerity of dreams.

The Blind

Gunners a decade dead
wing through my father's mind
as he limps out to the blind
bundled against the wind.

By some ancestral code
fathers and sons don't break,
we each carry a load
of which we cannot speak.

Here we commit our dead
to the unyielding land
where broken windmills creak
and stricken ganders cry.

Father, the dog, and I
are learning how to die
with our feet stuck in the muck
and our eyes trained on the sky.

Elegy for Diktynna

Go if you must, and swim
the dim waters of Acheron
    for Actaeon.

When my engraved grouse gun
passes to someone else's son,
    I'll whistle "Come."

Air

Come Diktynna come—
once more the mourning dove
coos in the blooming plum.

Mark the wood duck drake
plummeting through a grove,
and greenheads in the brake.

When fledglings try their wings
and waves of migrants heave
skyward in widening rings,

you will not heed my gun
nor leave this grassy grave—
your hunting days are done.

Drowse Diktynna drowse
lulled by a humming hive
under the apple boughs.

So stealthily stole death
my love could not retrieve
your evanescent breath.

II. ELMWOOD'S MAUD GONNE

To Eat, or Not to Eat

And there came a voice to him,
"Rise, Peter; kill, and eat."
                    —Acts X, 13

I. Brother Fox

A windless cloudless night
refroze the puddled ice
where geese chose to alight.
Waking at dawn they found
their feet webbed to the pond.
Drawn by their doleful cries
a fox strolled from the wood
with mayhem in his eyes.

II. Whitetails

Hoofed rats that they are,
they live in cervine fear
of carnivores who dine
on tenderloin of deer
or crown rack of fawn
downed with a young red wine.

III. Little Heart Butte

Grouse peck at its breast
and pheasants at its foot.
Buffalo berries west
and Russian olives east
girdle this shortgrass butte,
this table set for a feast.
I, the unbidden guest,
have little heart to shoot.

A Gun Dog
Named Maud Gonne

She no longer hears
whistle or wings.
The drums in her ears
were delicate things.

There will be water
to gun when she goes,
autumns of slaughter,
winters to doze,

pups to apprise
what fencerows yield,
but never so wise
a nose in the field.

Hunting Time

It's not just dirt-cheap prices,
diseases in our herds
or the global banking crisis.
Our fields are beset by birds.
Gwynn slips in a cartridge,
and another shell is pinned—
poets and dogs and partridge
all working into the wind.

The raptor is our fellow
predator of the air.
We humans lack his yellow
iris, his slitted stare;
but Brownings are as deadly
as dripping beak or claw,
and our prey bleeds as redly
as rodent eaten raw.

Though nowadays a shooter
keeps impulse under lock,
my old Kentucky tutor
once shot and stuffed a hawk.
He told me time was reckoned
by the crippled bird's last breath
as the marksman spared a second
to practice for his death.

The Recruit
Memorial Day, 1997

An honor guard of battle-scarred old men
discharges antique carbines at the sky
as though the ghosts of war were winging by
like pintails flushing from an ice-rimmed fen.
How many of these troops will hunt next fall?
Fewer and fewer totter out to shoot.
They hardly hear the mallard's bugle call
which lures me to the sloughs with my recruit—
a boy shouldering arms where reeds grow tall
and mankind's present enmities are moot.

Labrador & Pintail

Unposted

Abandoned where the grass grew lank and damp,
the antiquated grain drill seemed a toy
some Lilliputian farmer might employ
to plant a field small as a postage stamp.

Kelly opened a hopper filled with seed
nutty and sweet as Wheaties in the bag.
Where were the plowman and his plodding nag
to run that good grain through the metered feed?

Flushed from a pigweed patch, a pheasant sailed
over the leafless tree row flecked with red
where shrunken apples hung unharvested
or fallen to the stubble, lay impaled.

Squinting into the distance, Kelly said
"It was the farmer, not the seed what failed."

Game Log

"Learn now the lore
of living creatures."
A *clowder* of cats
cheerfully chases
a *charm* of finches,
a *rabble* of robins.
A *shoal* of fishes
frantically flees
a *pod* of seals
or a *gam* of whales.
A *pack* of pointers
flushes from bushes
a *bevy* of quail
or *covey* of partridge
while hunters are pestered
by *swarms* of hornets,
clouds of mosquitoes,
and *hordes* of wardens.
A *gaggle* of geese
dabble and gabble,
as aimless as auks
or a *plague* of poets.

The Steward

Lord, thou deliveredst unto me
five talents; behold, I have gained
five talents more.
     Matthew XXV, 20

Pheasants and sharptail grouse
nest near his modest house.
Pronghorn antelope
graze on a Rosebud slope.

Morris no-till drills
pulled by three Versatiles
keep the soil from blowing
off his communal hills—

hills that the bison haunted
and his Sioux forebears hunted,
fields where the cocks are crowing
and his green sons, growing.

The Cutting

Culled from a milling herd
a calf bawls at the sky,
and heifers question why
ponies were ever spurred.

Cowboy, colt and calf
all with their tails awry—
as though my dogs and I
ran roosters through the chaff

and made the feathers fly.

Tide Race

The wood duck's wood-pecked house
creaks in an April gust.
A drumming sharptail grouse
dances the grass to dust.

Round-bottomed as a boat
that sails his flooded fen,
whistling an alto note,
the cobb pines for his pen.

Gales rush from the south,
and geese at tailwind speed
seek the Mackenzie's mouth
to be the first to breed—

to stand watch at a nest
in Nunavut's Northwest.

Unnatural Selection

From orchard aisles they now traverse
a young doe and a slim spike-buck
observe their fecund mother nurse.
A year ago I watched them suck.

The old doe hobbles across our lane,
trailing her bloody afterbirth.
Two infants wobble in her train—
the latest scourges put on earth

to browse snap-dragons to the roots,
ravage the dogwood by our wall,
feast on newly-grafted shoots,
and feed archers when apples fall.

Birthday Dog

You are fourteen. Multiply by seven:
your age in human years is ninety-eight.
How long until you couch in canine heaven?
My one-time watchdog snores as children skate
circles outside her many-cushioned house.
Do you remember your two thousand doves,
pheasants and partridge, geese and sharptail grouse?
You were their mistress, they your scented loves—
feathery pillows when the hunt was done—
and I? I was your double-barreled gun.

Huntress

for Dan Treat D.V.M.

Her first bird was a crippled mourning dove.
   She somersaulted down a ditch
     head over heels in love,
buttoned her bird and bounded up the pitch.

Her first drake dropped beyond a refuge sign.
   Wriggling under the lowest wire,
     she swam a perfect line
as though posting a proof of her desire.

Her first goose gave her nose a nasty peck.
   Battered by its unbroken wing
     she leapt to grab its neck
and growling, drag it back for me to wring.

Her first loss was her superhuman ear.
   Hand-signalled on each unmarked run,
     she could no longer hear
whistling wingtips; even at last, the gun.

At fourteen she was walking into walls,
   fouling the carpet, losing teeth.
     Farewell to mallard calls
and decoy spreads, wild roosters on the heath.

To St. Francis of Fargo fell the chore,
   the Nembutol a gentle thrust
     to launch her from our shore.
The last look in her fearless eye was trust.

Perro del Amo

Go where the blue wings flash
over the whitecapped wave,

where crippled mallards splash
and every bitch is brave.

When the returning dove
roosts at your mother's grave,

I'll bury a box of ash
beside her in the sod.

Vaya con Dios, love,
you were the dog of God.

III. ELMWOOD'S BOLD FENIAN

Prairie Hunt

Missouri Breaks

I am a trespasser on treeless ground,
home to the sharptail and the furtive Hun,
and here the tallest thing for miles around
is a small hunter shouldering his gun.

A blooded dog quarters the feral rye,
and my body's long quarrel with my mind
is silenced by a landscape and a sky
legible as a Bible for the blind.

The Great Chain of Eating

Last night I heard the vast mosquito hatch.
Now big brown dragonflies swarm from the wood,
circle above our apple trees and snatch
mosquitos hungering for human blood.
Gorging on dragonflies, the swallows swoop
until the peregrine perceives her prey
darting below. She folds her wings to stoop,
smashing a swallow in a puff of gray.

So in Montana, when I lofted flies,
brookie, brown or cutthroat trout would rise,
fat with the blood of bugs that fed on mine.
I poached my catch beneath a lodgepole pine
and cached my fishbones far, far from the camp
to foil the bears. Then lit my Coleman lamp.

Too Old For This Game

I flushed six roosters from a frozen slough
and knocked one down with barrel number two.
Wingtipped by a Federal .20 shell,
a pheasant cock can always race like hell.
The drift rose cattail-tall in the marsh's lee.
I broke through crust. Chest-deep, I paddled free.
Feeney, gone wild with tracking so much scent,
couldn't imagine where our cripple went.
In knee-high snow we charged most of a mile,
pitting our wind against the rooster's guile;
then, triumphant, I trudged back to the truck
with bird in vest by dint of dog and luck.
I kenneled up my son of a champion bitch,
gutted the cock, and threw up in the ditch.

Long Shot

It flushed wild and swung so far ahead
that turned downwind it didn't look much bigger.
The F150 length by which I led
was perfect for my Parker's full-choke trigger.
The magnum lead haloed around the red,
ring-necked cock to which Bold Fenian sped.

I've had no store-bought meat for thirteen weeks.
In autumn I subsist on what I shoot,
fast-flying roosters armed with spurs and beaks
that Feeney finds and fetches to my boot.
Our pheasant casseroles are much adored.
"Rule the birds of the air," saith the Lord.

Ducks Lose, Pheasants Gain

Mudholes I used to wade for wingshot drakes
    pass beneath the plough
or harbor grouse and pheasant cocks that now
    dust-bathe in prairie lakes.
Drought can come on so swiftly, heading wheat
    dries to worthless straw.
What ails this wind-bedeviled land, what flaw
    brings unrelenting heat?
What thirst draws down the wells, unclouds the sky?
To ask is to invite a facile lie.

Salsola Kali

Farmers taught me to see our tumbleweeds
   as wind-driven grain drills
   sowing their hated seeds
in every furrow that the tractor tills.
Russian thistles rolling across our hills:
   they grant the upland bird
   which cannot speak a word
in their defense, the nesting place she needs.

Snowgeese
for Charles Beck

The flock is whorled like a translucent shell
and intricate as the tubing of a horn,
its embouchure, the soft foot of a snail
lighting on sand, except the sand is corn,
chisel ploughed and left to build the soil
from which indebted farmers have been torn.

I catch one note—a wild, wayfaring cry
as snow geese splash into a glacial mere.
Framed by moraines under a nacreous sky,
they echo in the chambers of my ear.
How does an ear rival your artist's eye
that sees what I can only hope to hear?

Ischemic Event

The mirrors where the mallards come meant sloughs,
and *rooster wagon* was the hunting car
rushing him to the hospital ER.
My backseat labrador was *Drooling Flews*
and a long wingshot, *Father never choke.*
Told of the metaphors by which he spoke
he laughed "At long last I have met my Muse."

Hunter's Log
for William Huber

I. The Peacemaker

I reach Oahe via the Grey Goose Road,
crossing the dammed Missouri headed west,
a lawsuit weighing on me like a load
carried too long, from which I long to rest.
An eagle swooping down the gullied slopes
races the Bronco as though Rosebud bound.
There the fulfillment of my partners' hopes
depends upon one hunting friend I've found.

A Rosebud Sioux topping three hundred pounds
and six feet five, Bill fills the barroom door.
One chamber clear, his cannon holds five rounds—
Colonel Sam Colt's persuasive .44.
Showing it off, he tells me with a smirk,
"Always go armed. Fighting is too much work."

Mad Mary's Saloon, Pierre, SD

II. Bronco

You don't look right with all your mud washed off,
your blood-stained rugs shampooed, your shine restored.

No more than I'd sound right without the cough
owed to my smokes and all the booze I've poured.

"Whose wheels are these?" my hunting buddies scoff.
Women are from GM; and men, from Ford.

III. Double

Two flapping roosters are a heart attack
that fells me every time except today.
They flush. I fire. Headshot, they tumble smack
into the swamp where Feeney earns his pay.
A bowl of steak tartare, a bed of down?
Or blue eyes fathoming two eyes of brown.

IV. Each Other's Measure

Suddenly we heard the sound of barking—
the snuffling nose that pheasant hunters prize—
the labrador, quartering, flushing, marking.
I glimpsed the wolfish hunger in your eyes

as Feeney zigzagged through the rows of trees,
kicking out flustered hens on either side.
From the dry switchgrass whispering at my knees
two roosters vaulted skyward, and they died.

For my part I admired your untilled fields,
sunflower stalks, wheat stubble holding snow,
each drop of moisture that a winter yields
hoarded to make your desert seedlings grow.

I judged your farming as you judged my hunting,
and neither fellow found the other wanting.

V. To John Murphy

The flushing rooster is a thrill
  greater than any kill
in which we've taken part or ever will

until the hunting boots of God
  tamp us under the sod
and all the pheasants that we've missed applaud.

Wagging their tails, our dogs will tell
  the other labs in hell,
"They killed in order to have hunted well."

VI. Fourth Time Pays For All

We named him Battlecock—
lord of the fields and fens,
head cock of the walk,
pride of the roosting hens.

As one would stalk a buck
with ten tines on his rack,
we chased him in the muck.
Each time we struck his track

he flushed far from the gun,
crowing as he fled
Bold Fenian on the run
and Murphy wasting lead.

Feeney and I have won.
The Battlecock is dead.

Flushing Roosters

VII. Feeney's Christmas

We sneaked into the corn.
They flushed out at the end,
cocks cackling in their scorn
for man and his best friend.

Trudging back to the Ford
I swung round with an oath
as two young roosters soared
and Lord! I drilled them both.

My puppy's Christmas presents
lay flopping in the ditch,
a brace of fragrant pheasants.
Feeney had struck it rich.

VIII. Season's End

A wingshot pheasant, downed but not undone:
with so much cattail slough for you to scour
your last retrieve lasted for half an hour.

Smoking a cigarette, I breeched my gun,
patient until I saw your rooster cower
cornered and humbled by a higher power.

IX. Return to the Rosebud

Sam Gwynn, that artful chef and sonneteer
    flies north to shoot next year
    and steep our quarry in
his marinade of juniper and gin.

Out hunting we'll hear whines from the pickup box
    as loafing pheasant cocks
    roost in the leafless trees
or strut through wheatgrass curried by the breeze.

"Cry havoc and let slip the dogs of war!"
    Feeney and his friend Thor
    will quarter a ravine,
articulated halves of a machine.

Fragrant as Minnesota conifers,
    the stunted junipers
    men and retrievers walk
will mask the scent of every bird we stalk.

Will roosters that we flush in range fall dead,
    shot through the heart or head
    by poets who, alas,
can hardly hit a heifer in the ass?

Our trophies field-dressed and our charges fed
    in Huber's Chevy bed,
    the weary will convene,
all thoughts turned to Professor Gwynn's cuisine.

When prairie dogs are rolling up their town
    just as the sun goes down
    and Mars flares into view,
the zenith will be juniper berry blue.

Ecce Canis

From the first slough some forty birds flushed wild.
    Maddened by pheasant scent,
    Bold Fenian was with child
while I triangulated where they went.

North to the mallards' frozen mating hole,
    a second cattail slough
    rimming a bullrush bowl,
we hunted, panting as the pheasants flew,

all but their patriarch who fell stone dead.
    I watched his grandson go,
    a gutshot cock that sped
to switchgrass tufted in the distant snow.

Under those drifts our harder hunt began.
    Eluding every cast
    it burrowed, bolted, ran
until at last Fenian pinned it fast.

I floundered to a roadside willow stand,
    collapsing on a log
    where Feeney licked my hand.
Unworthy man, behold thy hunting dog.

Missing Mass

He hath put a new song in my mouth.
Psalm 40:3

Going to church afield
I bear the Decalogue
as St. Michael, his shield.
My faithful altar dog
precedes me up the aisle,
mile after dusty mile.

A gale sweeps through the choir
and dries the prostrate grass
lightning and prairie fire
forge to beaten brass.
Tinted anew each day,
the dome is blue or gray.

The blood of every bird
I sacrifice this fall
let me translate to Word,
responses to the call
that asks us to record
a new song to the Lord.

Soul of the North

Out of my depth, I pray.
Bound as I was at birth
to fish, to hunt the earth
and find my northern way,
I mutter "I have sinned,"
wander the wild grass,
flourish awhile and pass
whistling into the wind.

As char swim to the clear
tundra rivers that run
under the midnight sun,
as wolves follow the deer
drawn from ford to ford,
as clamorous geese in V's
throng to the thawing seas—
all creatures of one accord—
my soul thirsts for the Lord.

Night Flight

Downward to darkness on my muffled wings
I hunt the wintry silence of a dream
whose spell is shredded by a rabbit's scream,
the coldest, purest note creation sings.
Femur and fur strewn at a supper's end:
bon appetit, Reynard, rival and friend.

Fieldmice and frantic voles submit to law
whose statutes I administer in sleep,
ruling my fields and barnyard by the deep
authority vested in beak and claw.
Focussing yellow irises, I prowl
in the infrared spectrum of the owl.

Checklist

Cheetos and chocolate chips for Tim to nibble,
a shrinkwrapped pound of Jimmy's jerkied deer,
a sixpack of nonalcoholic beer,
for Feeney's sake a Ziplock bag of kibble,

my Thompson .410 pistol underneath
the driver's seat; towrope and jumper cables,
the Game and Fish sunrise and sunset tables,
my lockback Buck knife in its buckskin sheath,

Nitro Solvent, Rem Oil and cleaning rod,
boxes of Super X non-toxic shot—
can there be anything that I forgot?
The truck is packed. The luck I leave to God.

The Chase

Now then, Glaucon, we must post ourselves (we philosophers)
like a ring of huntsmen around the thicket, with very alert minds,
so that justice does not escape us by evaporating before us.

The Republic (432b)

I. November 24

I whirl at the faint thunder of the flush,
snap off the safety, plant my backfoot boot,
   shoulder the gun but do not shoot.
One wing flails feebly in the falling hush

as the bird swerves across the frozen bog.
It flaps about five rods, glides to the ground,
   leaps skyward with a second bound
foiled by the canines of an airborne dog.

Here is the cock I winged two weeks before,
its crop crammed full of leavings from the corn,
   its loss a disappointment borne,
but bird in mouth, the settling of a score.

The neck snapped is a mercy long deferred.
When our Alberta clippers start to blow
   no slow starvation in the snow,
no fox or coyote will consume this bird.

I bear our trophy to the truck in bliss,
the proud retriever frisking at my knees.
   Glaucon hunting with Socrates
could hardly have been happier than this.

II. December 8

Cascading from the cropland's terraced shelf,
the sidehill western wheatgrass rolls away
and the seedheads of sideoats grama sway,
descending to the deadend basin's shore.
The closest roadhead is a mile or more.
"Think like a rooster, Tim," I tell myself.

Black-eyed susans have colonized the slopes,
feral reminders of the sunflower fields
abandoned when the weevils halved our yields.
In the foodplots whose flanking grasses drain
to clumps of cattail topped by feathery cane
two practiced predators repose their hopes.

Windward we work to maximize surprise.
Four miles into this prairie white with hoar
Feeney pounces. Two lurking roosters soar
and fall victim to stamina and stealth,
weighting my vest with other-worldly wealth,
a pair of cocks purloined in paradise.

Contemplating the eldest of our arts,
I gut the birds and feed my friend their hearts.

III. December 15

I pick my slow way past the pockmarked sedge
     where calves have left their divots,
then climb to hunt the upland's grassy edge
     rounding the center pivots
  whose verdant verge I choose to stalk.
There breakfast lies within a rooster's walk.

The prairie is a poem rarely read.
     Its looseleaf pages blow.
Too many students of this landscape fled
     its poverty and snow.
  Today I limp on stiffening knees,
hoping that heedless pheasants take their ease

in pigeon grasses sprung from durum stubble,
     in fragrant cedar shadow
where a boy watched his father down a double.
     Maker of marsh and meadow,
  grant me more time to understand,
more years to walk and memorize this land.

Mourning Doves

The Blind Retrieve
for Steve Syrdal

I. Training

He won his ribbon. Last night as it grew dark
I fired the launcher dummy into stubble.
He strained and barked but made a perfect mark,
taking his flawless line. Then ran a double.

He whirled and stopped dead on a whistle blast,
knowing his third, last trial was the blind.
He charged dead downwind on Steve's signaled cast
as if he knew by heart the handler's mind.

Grimly, I ran a quarter mile this morning
with Feeney grinning ear to ear beside me,
loping beside the slow man he was scorning.
Ingrate, had *he* the stature to deride me?

Eight years ago, his wobbly legs were rubber,
hopelessly short. No muscle to his hinders,
he was a butter tub of puppy blubber
and mark? Mark? He should have been wearing blinders.

Feeney, we'll run for half a mile tomorrow.
The doves, yes! The Canadian doves are coming
whom you'll retrieve from every fallow furrow
and grouse? The shortgrass, sharptail cocks are drumming.

II. Scotch Triple

Feeney was loping with a dove in jaw
just as I downed three birds with double barrels.
Then it was Dead Bird, Back! Lay down the law,
and put to rest all of our summer's quarrels.
We were in acorns, like a pair of squirrels.

III. Challenge

Challenge: handler has four doves on the ground,
dog driven crazy by explosive sound
and glimpse of carnage raining from the air.
Double a pair. Reload. A second pair,
breathe while a birdless sky grants a reprieve.
Sunflowers, worse than corn. The blind retrieve.

IV. Blow Sand Theatrics

Feeney, why are you limping on three legs,
sadly stumbling, a woeful clown who begs
sympathy from your audience of one?
Give me that paw while I lay down my gun.
Lie down, down, down! Don't bite, you little bastard!
Roll over, don't you know you're over-mastered?

Poor cripple, you've been lured by wicked doves
to Mexican sand burrs, and I have no gloves,
no pliers. Love, were I a few years older,
I couldn't hoist you on my scrawny shoulder
and, to your Canis Minor, play Orion,
though once I played Androcles to a lion.

V. Drain Eleven

Two fathers with two eight-year-olds in tow
stand stranded at Cass County Drain Eleven,
marooned in rubber boots: "How many?" "Seven."
The beans were solid seeded, ten inch row.

No dog. The fathers, heroes to little kids
who watched those doves downed into trackless crop,
welcome an old handler who calmly bids
a trained retriever to each dead bird drop.

Feeney, wasted, had nailed his fifteenth dove.
He rolled out of his kennel with a groan,
but children are his rarely sated love,
and each forsaken dove, he makes their own.

VI. Harvest Moon

A year ago Steve saw me in seizure's throes
and told his wife he'd bidden goodbye to Tim.
Frank Miller gave me the last rites, and Frank knows,
Christ's priest that he is, when eyes go dim,
pulse slows, blue takes the fingers and the toes,
pray for the soul.
               Tonight a full moon rose
and sang over my head a harvest hymn.

Posted

Drive with caution. This township strip of gravel
is much impeded by a herd of pheasants
    flaunting their adolescence,
and it is posted thus: Restricted Travel.

Beside me is an unmowed stretch of meadow
Feeney and I were tempted by all summer.
    One month hence some Hummer
will cast over this grass its massive shadow

as herds of Fargo bankers, lawyers, brokers,
who have shelled out their seven hundred dollars
    on GPS collars
which pointers wear like diamond-studded chokers,

hunt on this land I once farmed to perdition.
God bless the rich. I was one and I know 'em
    and say to them this poem
without a hint of malice or sedition:

Hunter and lab will walk and flush some pheasants,
strolling without our double-barreled Browning,
    the one who isn't clowning
awed in September by an August presence.

Three Seasons
for L.G. and S.C.

Feeney the fragrant—
his black coat browned by pond scum,
reeking of birdblood.

My rubber kneeboots
shedding mud in the closet,
cocklebur heaven!

My thirsty Bronco—
choking on pheasant feathers
late in November.

Forty some roosters
cleaned and bagged in the freezer?
Good until Easter.

The Brummond Quarter

I.

Into the wind and frosted grass we quartered.
So many hens were roosting on that prairie,
that Bricks for Brains (both of his ears were mortared)
raced at a pace no whistle blast could vary
until we reached a slope of silverberry.

A rooster Feeney missed leapt up behind me.
It fell, leaving behind a cloud of feathers.
Sunrise doing its level best to blind me,
I watched my lab coursing through canes and heathers,
waving his black flag high above his withers.

Chasing it down, he fetched it to his master,
who sat high on a hillside, smoking, panting.
This hunt which started out such a disaster,
dog run amock, a hunter raving, ranting,
was now a blessing, leaving nothing wanting.

II.

Minutes later I stood beside my truck.
Afield, Steve told me that he'd had no luck,
only some merry points on flushing hens.
But then I watched him whip round in the fens,
zigzag behind his dogs into the wind
and pound the pterodactyl they had pinned.
Unvested, it was the largest bird I'd seen
since the first cock I missed at age thirteen.

III.

Crippled by an inflamed Achilles' heel,
I've wrong-footed the plowing. So I kneel,
pry off my boot, massage my tortured foot
much as a scrub oak bends to mend its root.
When Steve returns, with never a sight of cock,
from flushing hens after his three mile walk,
I limp into the canebreak, tall rice grass
that lures descending pheasants as they pass.
A loafing lurker leaps up from the cane.
Twisting my right foot in my whimpered pain,
I break the rooster's right leg with my gun.
Into the swamp Steve and his bitches run,
another flush. Death at the second shot.
The swamp monster? No longer *is,* but *not,*
cornered in cattails, blasted from the air,
gutted, quartered, diced for the gumbo pot.
Tag-teamed. Three dogs, two men. Death isn't fair.

A Pair of Roosters

Cole

Cole is now six feet three.
So small, slender was he,
his unshaven cheek so tender,
I gave him a girl's gun,
a thirteen one-eighth pull
fitting his winter wool.
Most every shot rang true.
Down dropped the mallard drake,
down wailed the wingshot gander
Feeney plucked from the lake.
I gave him a grade four gun
left by father to son,
in hopes I'd produce my own;
I gave him a Buck sheath knife
and an old Arkansas stone
on which a kid could hone
the dull sides of his life.
A blond, blue-eyed boy,
stockpad fitted to shoulder,
he hadn't far to travel
to gain his mastery
of stubble, slough or tree,
just a few miles of gravel,
a few years to grow older.

Rhymes from the Rosebud

I only hold this land in trust.
—William Huber

My bones are those of a deer
frightened by fang and claw,
but you are built like the bear
who downs a longhorn steer
with one swipe of his paw,
and you could devour me raw.

Cottonwoods by the creeks
and scrub oaks in the draws,
cedars the mule deer seeks,
wild plum the rooster claws:
only ten years ago
I stumbled on your land.
I've hunted it in snow,
winds I could just withstand.
*

*indicates poem continues on the following page

From miles away I'd know
your bin site on this ridge.
Twelve thousand years ago
your forebears crossed a bridge
where now the Bering Sea
pummels a Russian shore.
Dream of those rocks with me.

William, I have learned more
of *heartbeat* in the hunt
here than I've learned at home,
as has my barking runt.
Down Collins Creek I roam,
learning not just the land
where deer and water flow,
but from the mind and hand
of him who keeps it so.

Georgic

for Bryan Stotts, District Ranger

This is the shoreline of a glacial lakebed.
Some of its flora, fauna are endangered.
Not so the leafy spurge, vile interloper,
the milkweed strewing cotton to the breezes.
Not so the cottonwoods or dwarfish scrub oaks,
the white-tail deer that multiply like chipmunks.
Here autumn daubs its trees above the stockponds
by fours or fives. We have no soaring forests,
just refuge for the wild, pinnated chickens
on a last vestige of the tall grass prairie,
a gift the cattle graze and take as granted.

Feeney flushes a frantic, dustpan dancer
from silverberry bushes in these sandhills,
the blown dunes of the Sheyenne National Grassland
where so much rain has fallen this October,
that tall grasses binding erosive hillsides
are succulent and seeding out of season.
In a damp oxbow looping by the Sheyenne
I once dug up a white-fringed prairie orchid,
fragrant by night, pollinated by sphynx moth
or butterfly, the rare Dakota skipper.
Potted it for my mom. It promptly perished.

*

Spare this land my trowel and the ploughshare.
Broken for barley in the Nineteen Twenties,
a decade later much of it was moonscape,
now colonized by stands of quaking aspens,
each of those clumps a single organism.
Feeney and I shall trace our tracks come April
when the pooled hollows trill with hatching peepers,
when ferns unfurl their fronds in every gully,
grasses and forbs turn sunshine into fodder,
when calves that boys can sling over their shoulders
nuzzle the udders of their mooing mothers.

Prairie Chicken

Flight to Murdo
for Father Lance Oser

He fled the flooding Red
which choked on ice and snow,
and how far did he go?
To a Best Western bed
four hundred miles away,
two thousand feet higher.
God knows, were he a flyer,
he would go there each day
just as the winter wheat
reclaims its tint of green—
a change of heart, of scene,
a refuge, a retreat.

He saw ten thousand geese
staging, the roadside pheasants.
Then begged a prairie presence,
"Grant that our birds increase."
He glassed a rolling reach
of cows that tourists pass.
Calf frisking in the grass,
he was renewed, but speech?
Let me just say the slope
of grassland where he parked,
each pasture that he marked
was crazed by antelope.

Miles to Go

Mile four twenty, eighty to go to Fargo,
heavy flurries, the gale less than force seven,
driving conditions well shy of full blizzard.
What has become of me, instinct and reflex,
night vision? Whiteblinded by truckers' headlights
and frightened as I haven't been for decades,
I've no shovel, no sleeping bag or tow rope,
no skis, no stove, only two squares of chocolate.
Well, if we hit the ditch, there's Feeney's kennel,
we can curl up, and he can be my sled dog.
At least I'm not tanked on a pint of whiskey,
though I would kill to have one in my glovebox.

Fin de Saison

This is our second blizzard in six days.
Last night the sun sank through a high cloud haze
just as a rooster tried to run the road.
Jammed in a double copper-plated load,
leapt from the hand-braked Ford still on the go.

Feeney lunged through the ditch to drifted grass,
quartering faster with each zigzag pass.
Eighty yards distant in that 'sessile hush',
I glimpsed a fleck of red, a busted flush
and a black gymnast blasting from the snow.

A flightless cripple armed with razor spurs
grimly gripped in his jaws, four cockleburrs
pinned to his shoulder like a *croix de guerre,*
Feeney returned with a triumphant air,
his season finished. Let the blizzards blow.

IV. EPILOGUE: A HUNTING SEASON

Shotgun, Whistle and Shells

Weapon of Choice

My rifle far outweighed my fishing rod.
It was a bolt action .22
that couldn't stop a bear or wolf attack
loosed on our campsite by an angry God.
The rod? I lashed it to my Boy Scout pack,
    and oh what trout we poached
    after my wrist was coached.
The bears were easy. Raise your arms and roar
    Milton, <u>Paradise Lost</u>, Book II.
I've wrecked five rods. The .22? Like new,
unlike my twenty gauge, its action loose,
    shedding its threadbare screws
    from forty years' hard use,
a weapon I adore more than my booze.

The Blown Hunt

I had a sneezing seizure yesterday.
  Now I'm supposed to hunt,
  but I shall have to punt,
my lower back is in such disarray.

Today my own garage seems far away.
  How did a simple sneeze
  so fell me to my knees
that all my best-laid plans *gang aft agley*?

Feeney pouts in his kennel in dismay.
  Picture ten thousand acres
  with few if any takers
and more targets than any man could slay.

He dreams of sharptails on their bales of hay
  watching the rising sun,
  their coloration dun,
or dancing little dust clouds from the clay.

Working Dogs

I am in awe of guide dogs for the blind
trained to lead their masters through endless nights
where no one with a tapping cane can find
his way to safety. To sit for traffic lights.

Next come the dogs employed by the police,
by special forces, sniffers-out-of-drugs
and bombs, the dogs of war handlers release
to combat terrorists and common thugs.

Then the Blue Heelers, herders of our sheep,
hemming a flock and moving it en masse
as blizzards close the heights. The trail is steep
to the lush valley and its winter grass.

Then there's the Labrador. With four ducks down
he marks and claims the swimmer, then the dead.
He tracks the wing-clipped pheasant through the brown
cattails, and all he asks is board and bed.

God gave the Saint Bernard the little keg
of cognac collared to his massive neck.
He digs the skier with a broken leg
from splintered pines that avalanches wreck.

Blessed be the wolf cubs in their den, the man
who nursed those mewling orphans in his cave
and gave them all the love a hunter can,
helped them to hunt, to herd, even to save.

Permission Granted

Woodbury Farms. Last year's first blizzard blew
brown clouds of pheasants over these fields. They flew
from corn to cattails, quarters posted up
tight as the rear end on a starving pup.
Seeking permission is a dreaded task
for most hunters, but me? Happy to ask,
having a sure-fire trick: let Feeney out
and start reciting puppy poems. Doubt
gives way to disbelief and then to laughter
as we gain access to the grass we're after.

Blond and blue-eyed, a boy leaps from his tractor.
Redford could cast him as his leading actor
in Grapes of Wrath Redux. The young man's smile
lights up the pasture and the silage pile.
I start out with an expert observation
on the harsh facts of cow-calf operation.

His father tools up on his ATV,
and soon we're all chuckling at poetry.
I give them Set the Ploughshare Deep, my book
set in the counties where they ranch. They look
at Beck's woodcuts, my clinchers, and perceive
through Charlie's eyes the *Ghost Farm* where men grieve,
the miracle of his *Snow Geese*. Says the son,
"Sir, you'll be welcome soon as Deer is done."

Consolation

Fenian, you winded your favorite smell,
    crashing through chest-high brush
    in falling snow, to flush
two cocks my stuck safety has saved from Hell.

" Kennel!" I hide a warm bird in the sod,
    staging a blind retrieve
    in which you so believe,
my whistle signals seem the Word of God.

Hunting on Thanksgiving

Thanks for my tall, Norwegian hunting buddy.
I love him best when his right hand is bloody
from gutting out our birds. Thanks for the true
friend you found me when I was twenty-two.
He flees from me, but I attach no blame
to Alan, who would never clean my game.

Thanks for the dog who frolics as I slog,
mud to my ankles, through this flooded bog.
Thanks for the pheasant stuffed into my vest
whose felling in these weeds was just a test
of heart pounding and fouled lungs out of breath.
Thanks for the priest who will attend my death.

Thanks for the bird I missed, for Feeney's flush,
the faint thunder of wings breaking the hush
of mass conducted in the open air.
Thanks for pulling me back from the despair
which might have lost me eighteen hundred days
I have devoted to my Maker's praise.

Prayer to St. Michael

Through tree rows flanked by harvested corn
where Gabriel winds his hunting horn,
through cattail sloughs where pups rejoice
with ardent boys, let me give voice
like a hound hot on the scent of a fox
to the art of hunting pheasant cocks
through wild grasses ungrazed by cattle.
Michael the Archangel, lead us in battle.

When farmers are finishing up their toil
and ploughs turn over the stubbled soil,
when whitetail bucks commence their rut
and squirrels are squirreling every nut,
when acorns fall from the scrub oak trees
and sunrise wakens the northwest breeze,
when leaves and limbs begin to rattle,
Michael the Archangel, lead us in battle.

Where hoar frost silvers the unhayed grass
and zigzag lines mark every pass,
where ringnecks tunnel out of view
and mallard wings are fringed with blue
and the doe sleeps in a switchgrass bed,
where green is gold, the reddest red
is Thomas Turkey's impressive wattle.
Michael the Archangel, lead us in battle.

Successor?

I. Going on Ten

Six inches of fluffy snow,
it is seven degrees below,
the wind from the West at seven—
 Labrador heaven.

On either side of the sun
the optical show has begun
with sundogs to left and right
 dazzling my sight.

Out of the waist-high grass
where Feeney and gunner pass
the pheasant cocks explode
 as I reload.

How long can Feeney keep up
this quartering with no pup
to back him in the field?
 When will he yield?

II. Stud Fee

Offered six hundred bucks
or first pick of a pup
which of them shall I choose?
Which of the litter sucks
hardest when puppies sup?
Who can untie my shoes?

III. Getting Acquainted

Tumbling him on his back
you throttle him by the throat.
Chubby as he is black,
black-hearted as his coat,

he longs to chew on your ear,
sneak kibble from your bowl
and sniff your rear, my dear.
Aren't puppies made to roll?

Too soon he will outsmart
and lead you through the slough.
But in his hunter's heart
he will never rival you.

To My Nephew

These farms bear patronymics. Here is Mairs',
the Hammer Half, Wes Alinder's, but pairs
of sloughs along this rutted lane I name
for a song's verses, "Too Old For This Game,"
"The Double," "Feeney's Christmas," and "The Blind."
Hunters and dogs long dead throng to my mind.

See where the marshes lap against the wood?
Capping that sea of grass, your grandpa stood
and executed birds your uncles missed.
Sixty yards out we'd watch a rooster twist,
fly four beats lungshot, fold wings and collapse,
a sacrifice in a cathedral's apse.

For now, Matthew, just learn to swing and shoot.
In every pothole where you sink a boot
you've sunk your roots, you've cached in memory
another autumn day; you hold in fee,
surer than any entry on a deed,
title to skies where ghostly pheasants speed.

Pass Shooter

Dedication is the privilege and torment of our species.

—Jose Ortega y Gasset

I.

Sciatica, a crushed cervical disk,
  the torn Achilles tendon in one leg—
"Let me sidestep the badger holes," I beg;
"no gain without a calculated risk."

A friend protests, "This is a young man's sport."
At grave danger of pitying myself,
  groaning, I stretch for ammo on my shelf.
"I can outfox them now," is my retort.

Each year miles-trudged-per-pheasant-cock declines
faster than does my tolerance for pain,
  for tangled sloughs, for blowing snow and rain.
The old dog sniffs my Winchester and whines.

II.

Long Tom Twelve, a gun for waterfowl
I haven't fired for years, is in my hand;
and last night's sugar snow has flocked the land.
"These back spasms are killing me," I growl.

Soybeans uncombined and the corn still green—
pheasants will forage in these crops all day,
unhuntable however hard we pray.
Last night from memory I mapped this scene.

Now I'm too lame to limp through birdless grass.
Flushing from their half-darkened slough to feed,
here flies the Ur-flock. With a canoe-length lead
I drop three in the ditches as they pass.

Sorry, Feeney—no lurkers holding tight
in cattails, no adrenaline, no rush
of blood brainward as pointed pheasants flush—
but fresh game for the Irish nuns tonight.

III.

I'd shot two cocks, and Feeney saw them drop.
Soybeans in rows, lanes on a running track
circled the slough as I was shouting "Back!"
and both ran scot free through the shelling crop.

Three days later, Syrdal, the Wrath of God,
brings in his bitches to reclaim the lost.
Chased from the slough, one pays the final cost.
Maggie solo tackles it in the sod.

Its mate was wing-tipped by an errant shot.
Three labradors are thinking, *Bird Alive.*
Bett, (by our clock nearly one hundred five,)
pins and retrieves. Steve says, "Waste not. Want not."

IV.

Meditations on Hunting: years ago,
corn strips, the winter food plots in these fields
held all the birds our Olson Section yields
when the ploughed soil is flecked with fallen snow.

Two brothers and their labrador, footworn,
worked to the wind. Their father capped the drive,
never quite so alert, quite so alive
as when his sons were coming through the corn.

Arthritic, diabetic, short of breath,
he'd seen the sun rise on a mallard blind.
Ortega y Gasset much on his mind,
his hunts were dress rehearsals for his death.

Fathers' Day

i.m. Vincent Murphy

Sunset, and mallards poured down on the pond.
You shot from a low saddle in the hills,
felling them like a wizard with his wand.
Hip-deep in loon shit, I retrieved your kills.

Ten years since absolution for your sins:
six children by your bed, aged eighty-three,
your last words to the family, "Vince wins."
Today our young priest speaks a homily

on God the Father and the Son he gave
to save this sorry world. We're told to pray
for every father resting in his grave,
for each child who is fatherless today.

Duck Shooting

NOTES

Songs of the North: Felsenmeer is frost-shattered granite. Brash is shattered, floating sea ice. Jacobshavn is a settlement on Greenland.

Diktynna Thea is an ancient Greek goddess of the hunt for whom I named my first lab. Unlike Actaeon, I was not torn to shreds by dogs for my impiety.

Hunting Time: The closing couplet is an allusion to R.P. Warren's "Bearded Oaks."

The Steward: is Bill Huber, a pioneer of no-till farming on the Rosebud Reservation in southwest South Dakota, and the dedicatee of my nine part Hunter's Log and of Rhymes from the Rosebud.

Tiderace: *Nunavut* is the name given to the enormous Inuit state carved out of the Northwest Territories.

Perro del Amo is Spanish for Dog of the Master or Dog of God.

Long Shot: An F150 is a full size Ford pickup, its length roughly the lead I needed on this shot.

Salsola Kali is the scientific name for a common tumbleweed, a species of wild amaranth.

"Snowgeese" is a masterful Charles Beck woodcut that prefaces the second section of my book, Set the Ploughshare Deep.

Hunter's Log: "Suddenly we hear the sound of barking" and "He kills in order to have hunted well" are both found pentameters I lifted from Ortega y Gasset's Meditations on Hunting.

Ecce Canis is Latin for 'behold the dog.'

ACKNOWLEDGEMENTS

The poems in the first two sections of this book are drawn from <u>The Deed of Gift</u> (Story Line Press, 1998), <u>Set the Ploughshare Deep</u> (Ohio University Press, 2000), and <u>Very Far North</u> (Waywiser Press, London, 2002). Many of the poems in the latter half of this book were just published in the double volume, <u>Mortal Stakes</u> and <u>Faint Thunder</u>, by this press. They have appeared in many periodicals. *The Hudson Review* published the nine poems in Hunter's Log, and The Chase. The Blind Retrieve, Posted, The Brummond Quarter, Rhymes from the Rosebud, and The Pass Shooter, have been printed in *Gray's Sporting Journal*. *Chronicles* published *Ecce Canis,* Huntress, Missing Mass, Soul of the North, *Fin de Saison,* Miles to Go, and many of the poems drawn from earlier books. *The New Criterion* published Cole. *First Things* published High Above Oahe and Georgics. *The Sewanee Review* published Unposted and Hunting Time. Other venues include *The Alabama Literary Review, The Dark Horse* in Scotland, *Light Quarterly, The Shit Creek Review* and *Chimaera* in Australia, *The Formalist, The Raintown Review, New Walk, On Second Thought,* and *Able Muse.*

I want to acknowledge Carl Altenbernd, proprietor of Gun Dog Kennels, trainer and breeder extraordinaire. Carl has trained all four of my labs and taught me much of what I've learned about handling these peerless partners. And I want to acknowledge Dan Ness, proprietor of Sheyenne River Kennels, Feeney's home away from home when I am traveling.

INDEX OF TITLES AND FIRST LINES

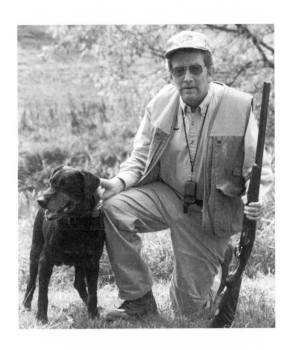

Born in 1951, Timothy Murphy grew up in the Red River Valley of the North and has hunted birds on the northern prairie since youth. He was graduated from Yale College as Scholar of the House in Poetry in 1972. His most recent collection of new poetry, published by The Dakota Institute Press, is *Mortal Stakes and Faint Thunder*, which also features the art of Charles Beck. Previous collections of poetry include *The Deed of Gift*, Story Line Press, 1998; *Very Far North*, Waywiser Press, 2002; and *Set the Ploughshare Deep*, Ohio University Press, 2002. With his late partner, Alan Sullivan, he translated the *Beowulf*, published by A B Longman in 2004.